CW00586865

South
African
Skies

South African Skies

KEITH GASKELL

Airlife
England

Acknowledgements

My 'mission' to photograph the aircraft of South Africa was made all the more enjoyable by meeting so many people who were willing to offer their assistance. I am particularly grateful to Robby Van Gelder and his colleagues at British Airways; Steve Duley, Jeanette Van Eck and the enthusiastic staff of Comair; Jeremy Labuschagne and Mike Litson of Court Helicopters; Hennie Delport of Phoebus Apollo; Mike Beachy Head of Thunder City Enterprises; Colonel Des Barker, Colonel Venter and First Lieutenant Burt Joubert of the South African Air Force; and Fred and Ian Cruickshank of the SAA Museum Society.

In addition to those listed above my sincere thanks to everyone who has supported this project in any way, especially Richard Church and my wife Maria for their advice, encouragement and long hours of proofreading.

The following publications proved to be valuable sources of information:

Air-Britain News
Australian Aviation
Aviation Letter
Flight International
Propliner Aviation Magazine
SA Flyer
The Aviation Hobby Shop's *Jet Airliner Production List* and *Turbo Prop Airliner Production List*
World Airnews for Continental Africa

Copyright © 2001 Keith Gaskell

First published in the UK in 2001
by Airlife Publishing Ltd

British Library Cataloguing-in-Publication Data
  A catalogue record for this book
  is available from the British Library

ISBN 1 84037 237 0

The information in this book is true and complete to the best of our knowledge. All recommendations are made without any guarantee on the part of the Publisher,who also disclaims any liability incurred in connection with the use of this data or specific details.

All rights reserved. No part of this book may be reproduced or transmitted in any form or by any means, electronic or mechanical including photocopying, recording or by any information storage and retrieval system, without permission from the Publisher in writing.

Typeset by Rowland Phototypesetting Limited, Bury St Edmunds, Suffolk
Printed in China

Airlife Publishing Ltd

101 Longden Road, Shrewsbury, SY3 9EB, England
E-mail: airlife@airlifebooks.com
Website: www.airlifebooks.com

Contents

Introduction

During the last decade South Africa has been warmly welcomed back to its rightful place in the community of world nations after years of conflict and isolation. A newly-found sense of national identity has begun to emerge and as this becomes stronger the 'New South Africa' will realise more of its enormous potential. Already tourism is flourishing as never before with visitors attracted by the spectacular scenery, the game reserves, resorts and beaches and the excellent food and wines. The country also has a vast store of mineral wealth upon which its traditional industrial and financial strength was founded and this continues to underpin the economy and provide much needed employment.

The development of aviation in South Africa during the last thirty years has, of course, been directly influenced by the country's political circumstances. During the years of international sanctions new aircraft were virtually unobtainable, so existing types had to be retained in service long after their retirement elsewhere in the world. Now the airports are alive with modern airliners and at long last the Air Force is receiving some new equipment. The result is that a unique mix of aircraft can now be found sharing South African skies, an exciting blend of veteran piston-engined transports, classic jet airliners, preserved supersonic fighters and increasing numbers of the latest civil and military types.

Johannesburg is the Republic of South Africa's largest city and main business centre, and a focal point for much of the region's aeronautical activity. At the International Airport modern airliners are very much in evidence with types ranging from small commuter turboprops through to the long-haul jets of major world airlines. Operating alongside these are the earlier generation Boeing 707s, 727s and BAC 1-11s and a varied selection of aircraft flown by freight haulers, charter companies and Government organisations. Other airports around Johannesburg, and its close neighbour Pretoria, provide a home base for companies which operate throughout southern Africa and for organisations which offer aircraft maintenance and conversion facilities. An unrivalled assortment of transport aircraft passes through these airports, with some types, such as the Andover, Caravelle and Viscount, unlikely to be seen anywhere else. A large and growing population of veteran Douglas Dakotas and Skymasters also operates from these airfields and a thriving preservation scene adds to the region's interest. The South African Historic Flight is well known for its wide-ranging DC-4 passenger charters and the South African Air Force Museum has an impressive collection of military aircraft, many of which are maintained in an airworthy condition.

A second centre of activity can be found seven hundred miles away on the country's south-western tip at the spectacular port city of Cape Town, where once again a growing selection of airlines share the International Airport with veteran transport aircraft. Cape Town's airport has, however, achieved world-wide fame in recent years because it is the home base for a unique collection of ex-military fast-jets. Excellent weather conditions and uncongested airspace have made Cape Town the ideal location for Thunder City Entertainments' operation which includes the world's only airworthy English Electric Lightning interceptors and Blackburn Buccaneer strike aircraft.

The photographs which now follow were taken by the author. They have been selected to give the reader a flavour for the exotic aircraft and colourful operators which can be found in this vast and beautiful country.

Scheduled-service Airlines

During the 1990s South Africa re-established itself as a prime destination and the region now displays the fastest rate of passenger traffic growth anywhere in the world. As a result, the number of airlines serving the country's airports rose rapidly and now around sixty offer scheduled services. Not surprisingly, over half are African airlines with most countries on the continent represented and six are locally-based South African airlines which operate in a fiercely competitive domestic arena. South African Airways (SAA), which is by far Africa's largest airline, is now profitable after many years in a steep decline and is preparing for its eventual privatisation. Looking further afield, airlines from the Middle East, the Far East and Australia are regular visitors and Europe is well served by the flag-carrier airlines of nine countries. The biggest market is to the United Kingdom which is contested by both British Airways and Virgin Atlantic as well as SAA. Although no American carriers serve South Africa directly, Delta's code-sharing arrangement with SAA on its services to Atlanta and New York offers travellers access to a large number of North American destinations. Whilst all of these airlines serve Johannesburg, several also fly on to Cape Town and to a lesser extent to Durban.

Left: South African Airways, which was created by South African Railways in 1934, built up a substantial long-haul network after World War Two and became an early operator of many new airliners including the Boeing 747-200 in 1971. However, severe operational difficulties were encountered throughout the 1980s as a result of South Africa's political isolation and the airline was barred from the airspace of most African countries until 1994. Since then it has re-established and expanded its links across the continent and by the turn of the century fifty airliners were in use serving thirty-seven cities in Africa, Europe, North and South America, India, the Far East and Australia. Swissair's parent SAirGroup acquired 20% of SAA during 1999 in the first stage towards eventual privatisation and alliances have been implemented with a range of international airlines. A new livery was introduced in 1997. The traditional orange and blue colours and flying Springbok symbol were replaced with a bold design based on the new national flag of the Republic of South Africa.

Above: SAA Boeing 747-300 ZS-SAJ wearing a special 1996 Olympic Games livery is towed to its stand at Johannesburg International. One of the airline's current priorities is to reduce the number of types in its diverse long-haul fleet, which was assembled in a piecemeal fashion over many years and includes several variants of the 747-200/300/400 and SP. The resulting combinations of different engine types, flight decks and interior layouts are expensive to operate and maintain, so a major order for replacement long-haul airliners is expected. A commitment in 1995 to order seven Boeing 777-200s was meant to start this process but those aircraft were never delivered.

Above: SAA was an early Airbus Industrie customer with its 1976 purchase of four specially modified A300B-2Ks for operations from Johannesburg Airport, which is 5,558 feet above sea level. They were joined by four A300B4s during the 1980s and seven A320s, all for use on the airline's domestic and regional services. These Airbuses have recently been replaced by twenty-one new Boeing 737-800s as SAA modernises its fleet and reduces the number of types in use. A300B-2K ZS-SDC *The Love Plane* landing at Johannesburg first entered service with the airline in January 1977.

Above: Boeing 737-200s have been operated by SAA since 1981/2 and will remain in service for several more years alongside a fleet of newly delivered 737-800s to operate domestic and regional services. Both types are flown by a single group of pilots thereby providing the airline with a significant cost saving.

Top opposite: South Africa is well served by a network of commuter and feeder services provided by two subsidiaries of SAA – South African Airlink and South African Express. South African Airlink has flown twenty-eight-seat British Aerospace Jetstream 41s since 1995 and operated a pair of Dornier Do228s until 2000.

Bottom opposite: ZS-NRH one of Airlink's sixteen Jetstream 41s, departs as sistership ZS-NRK taxies to its stand. Both were wearing the company's old SAA-style livery which was replaced by the airline's new corporate identity in 1999.

Above: ZS-NRK is shown again, this time in the new livery, but with Airlink Swaziland titles and modified fin markings. This Jetstream is used to operate scheduled services on behalf of the Swaziland Government as a replacement for bankrupt Royal Swazi National Airways. A period of significant expansion is now underway, as South African Airlink begins to take advantage of recent moves towards 'open skies' throughout Southern Africa. Thirty 37-seat Embraer RJ-135 regional jets are on order and options have been taken out for another forty which may be delivered as seventy-seat ERJ-170s.

Above: South African Express operates six de Havilland Canada DHC-8s and six Canadair CRJ-200ER Regional Jets. These modern fifty-seat airliners are flown in full SAA colours on routes which were unprofitable for the parent airline's larger aircraft.

Left: Comair, which was formed back in 1946 as Commercial Air Services, is now the second largest airline in southern Africa as well as the largest privately owned airline on the African continent. It became known as Commercial Airways or Comair in 1967 when limited scheduled services were introduced. Gradual expansion followed with a fleet of Dakotas and F-27 Friendships, but it was not until 1991 when the South African Government introduced airline deregulation that Comair was allowed to compete with SAA on the main domestic routes. Two Boeing 737-200s were acquired to operate a twice daily Johannesburg to Cape Town service and as other routes were added the fleet quickly grew. Five years later six 737s and two 727-200s operated domestic services linking Johannesburg with Cape Town, Durban and Port Elizabeth and international routes to Harare and Windhoek.

Comair's aircraft began to appear in British Airways colours during 1996 as a franchise agreement was implemented. BA had been looking for an airline to feed its London services with passengers from across southern Africa and was attracted by Comair's expanding network and many years of experience of the region. Since then growth has been rapid and Comair now carries one quarter of all South African domestic and intra-regional passengers. British Airways consolidated its interest in January 2000 by acquiring an 18.3% shareholding.

Comair leased two 142-seat Boeing 727-200s in 1996 for the busy Johannesburg to Cape Town route, where a larger aircraft was needed to provide a serious challenge to SAA. By 1999, six 727s were in service, all leased from Safair and each one displaying a different tail scheme from British Airways' catalogue of 'World Image' designs. The two examples depicted here are ZS-OBO with a *Benyhone* tartan design (*above*) and ZS-NOU with Danish *Flowerfield* art (*below*). These colourful images are now disappearing as BA reverts to the single and recognisably British identity illustrated on page 13. Perhaps surprisingly, given that 1,831 727s were built, Comair's are the only ones ever to have flown in full British Airways colours. Their days with the airline, however, are numbered as a more modern and efficient replacement is expected so that Comair can compete more effectively with SAA's new Boeing 737-800s.

Above: The ten Boeing 737-200s currently in Comair's fleet are used to operate domestic services and an expanding regional network. Outside of South Africa the airline serves Harare, Lilongwe, Lusaka, Victoria Falls and Windhoek and has plans to add other international destinations such as Nairobi and Ndola. In this photograph ZS-NNH, which was originally G-BGDH with British Airways, arrives at Johannesburg after operating one of Comair's ten daily services from Durban.

Above: Nationwide Airlines is a privately owned company which offers a low-fare alternative on some of South Africa's main domestic routes. A fleet of British Aerospace One-Elevens began to enter service in 1994 and within three years Nationwide was operating from Johannesburg to Cape Town, Durban, George and Port Elizabeth. Code-sharing agreements have been introduced with European carriers, the first one in March 1997 feeding traffic onto Sabena's Johannesburg to Brussels service, the second to Air Portugal's Lisbon service and more recently with Virgin Atlantic to London. One-Eleven-537 ZS-NUH displays the logos of Sabena and Air Portugal to promote these links. Nationwide has ambitions to operate its own long-haul services to Europe.

Right: Nationwide Air's first One-Eleven was ZS-NNM, a Series -400 'Combi' bought from Rolls-Royce in April 1994. This unusual One-Eleven is equipped with a large main-deck cargo door and strengthened floor and is used by the airline as a pure freighter to fulfil various cargo and mail contracts. Additional One-Elevens soon followed – six stretched Series -500s in 1994/5 and four Series -400s in 1996/7. The Series -500s operate in a spacious two-class configuration with twelve First and eighty-two Economy seats. The smaller Series -400 'pocket-rockets' have just seventy-two seats, which makes them particularly useful for the development of new routes. Apart from two aircraft in Central America, Nationwide's are now believed to be the last Series -400s used on scheduled passenger services.

Above: Three Boeing 727s joined the Nationwide fleet in 1996/7 including a passenger-configured 727-100 and a Series -100 freighter. The third 727 is a Series -200 ZS-ODO which can accommodate 149 passengers and is the airline's largest aircraft. The large Sabena titles illustrated were replaced with much less prominent markings in 1999.

Right: Nationwide Airlines began to acquire Boeing 737-200s to supplement its One-Eleven and 727 fleets during 1998. By mid-2000 five were in service including ZS-OMG, one of three from Croatia Airlines, and the two most recent additions which came from El Al.

Below: The sight of a Boeing 707 at airports around the world is becoming increasingly rare as operating restrictions, which are designed to limit noise, take their toll. Most of the survivors have been converted to freighters, leaving just a handful equipped to carry passengers. One example is Inter Air's ZS-IJI, an immaculate 1967-vintage Boeing 707-323C which still operates regular services from Johannesburg. Inter Air began operating in 1994 and uses a variety of Boeing 707/727/737 jetliners to operate scheduled and charter services throughout southern Africa and further afield. At the time of writing scheduled services were on offer from Johannesburg to Antananarivo, Douala, Libreville, Moroni, Ndola, Reunion and the Seychelles.

Since the initial steps towards deregulation were taken ten years ago South Africa's airline industry has grown significantly and competition on the main internal routes is now fierce. The most hotly contested route is between Johannesburg and Cape Town where an incredible forty daily round-trip services are now provided, using aircraft types as diverse as the Canadair Regional Jet, One-Eleven, 727, Airbus A300 and 747SP. Unfortunately the cost of operating these services has been very high – fuel being particularly expensive – and the inevitable result has been the failure of some airlines. The first casualty was Flitestar, an ambitious airline which began flying four Airbus A320s on domestic routes from its Cape Town base in October 1991. Flitestar eventually flew as far as Bahrain and had plans to serve Britain and Germany, but was unable to survive the lethal combination of high operating costs and low fares and went out of business in April 1994.

On 13 August 1999, Sun Air stopped flying, a victim of high costs and fare wars on domestic services. Sun Air was originally known as Bop Air, the national airline for the Republic of Bophuthatswana. It operated commuter airliners between Sun City and Johannesburg until the independent black national state was reintegrated with South Africa in 1994. The airline was reborn as Sun Air and established a network of scheduled domestic services operated by a fleet which grew rapidly to five Douglas DC-9-32s, five McDonnell Douglas MD-80s and a single Boeing 727-200 by 1998. Unfortunately, losses were also growing and after a long struggle to refinance the airline it ceased flying a year later. Boeing 727 ZS-NVR was transferred to Comair in 1999.

Taxiing in to park alongside Comair 727-230 ZS-NOV is Sun Air MD-82 ZS-OBF. Perhaps surprisingly, given the intense rivalry on South Africa's busy domestic routes, Comair owned 25% of struggling Sun Air.

Above: Aero Zambia was one of several attempts to establish new airlines to serve the country following the demise of Zambia Airways in 1994. Boeing 737-200C 9J-AFW was photographed at Johannesburg in January 2000, soon after Aero Zambia itself had ceased trading.

Left: Air Zimbabwe is a frequent visitor to Johannesburg with ten flights a week from Harare flown by the airline's fleet of three Boeing 737-200s and two 767-200ERs. Until recently the airline also served Cape Town and Durban but as a consequence of the unrest in Zimbabwe traffic has declined leading to the suspension of these services in June 2000.

Just about every national carrier from southern and central Africa can be seen in Johannesburg on a regular basis. Air Botswana's ATR-42s are frequent visitors, operating four daily services to nearby Gaborone. Unfortunately A2-ABB (*top*) was destroyed in tragic circumstances during October 1999 when the aircraft was stolen and deliberately crashed into two other ATRs. Thankfully there were no casualties other than the pilot himself. The airline quickly leased three ATRs from Air Littoral as a temporary measure until replacements could be acquired. F-GPYJ wears a modified version of the French airline's colourful livery during its lease to Air Botswana in 2000 (*above*).

Above: Air Malawi's sole Boeing 737-33A 7Q-YKP (which is also the largest aircraft on the Republic of Malawi register) departs Johannesburg on one of the airline's daily services, three of which go to Blantyre and four to Lilongwe.

Right: Boeing's magnificent 747SP ('Special Performance') is a shortened version of the basic 747, developed specifically to operate ultra-long range flights. South African Airways' six SPs were delivered during 1976/7 and became indispensable during the years of political isolation when flights were forced to make lengthy detours to avoid most African countries. They have also been leased to several African airlines for use in pioneering long-haul services to Europe. Air Namibia began operating long-haul services between Windhoek and Frankfurt in 1990, the year in which Namibia gained its independence from South Africa. An extension to London was added in 1992. Leased 747SP V5-SPF was used for many years to operate these services which are now flown by a 747-400 Combi acquired from Boeing in October 1999. Frequent services are also flown from Windhoek to Johannesburg and Cape Town, primarily with 737-200s but also with the 747.

Left: Boeing 747SP-44 ZS-SPA was painted in this distinctive African livery in 1995 when Alliance Air began operating from Dar es Salaam and Entebbe to London. The airline was created as a joint venture with SAA owning 40% and the rest shared between Air Tanzania and Uganda Airlines, the Governments of Tanzania and Uganda, and private investors. The idea was to build up long-haul services from Dar es Salaam and Entebbe which would be fed by domestic feeder services, but the various parties were unable to come to an agreement. The airline changed its name to SA Alliance Air and in an attempt to improve its results replaced the high-cost 747SP with SAA 767-200ERs in 1998 on the twice-weekly London services. Unfortunately the losses continued unabated and the airline stopped flying in October 2000.

Below: Another East African airline to adopt a local wildlife image for its livery is Air Tanzania, which paints a giraffe onto the tail of its aircraft. Boeing 737-33A 5H-TCA *Ngorongoro* is illustrated here arriving at Johannesburg after operating one of the airline's three-per-week services from Dar es Salaam.

Congo Airlines' smartly turned out Boeing 727-30 9Q-CRG *Ville de Goma* taxies to its stand at Johannesburg International at the end of a flight from Kinshasa and Lubumbashi, one of two services flown each week by the airline. This veteran airliner was actually the twenty-eighth 727 built, flying for the first time in February 1964 and delivered soon afterwards to Lufthansa to begin an exceptionally long and productive career. By the time this photograph was taken early in 2000 9Q-CRG had become one of the oldest 727s still in flying condition.

Egyptair serves Johannesburg three times a week from Cairo with a variety of aircraft from its diverse fleet such as this Airbus A340-200, SU-GBM. Although both cities are in Africa, the sheer size of the continent is demonstrated by the fact that flights between them take almost eight hours.

TAAG Angola Airlines operates three weekly services from Luanda to Johannesburg with Boeing 747-300 Combis or 737-200s. TAAG acquired its first 747 from Singapore Airlines in July 1997 and this was joined by an ex Swissair example (*above*) in 1999.

Most major European long-haul carriers, such as Iberia and Air Portugal illustrated here (*opposite*), maintain regular schedules to Johannesburg. The services operated by KLM, Lufthansa and Turkish Airlines continue on to Cape Town which is also served non-stop from Europe by British Airways, Virgin Atlantic and LTU. Most of these services arrive in South Africa during the morning after a long overnight flight and return northbound in the evening. In this late afternoon scene a selection of Airbus A340s and Boeing 747s await the nightly exodus to Europe (*above*). These two types dominate long-haul operations as the new generation of very large twin-jet Boeing 777s and Airbus A330s has yet to make much of an impact in South Africa.

Left: Singapore Airlines Boeing 747-400 9V-SMZ wearing 'Fiftieth Anniversary' markings departs Johannesburg en route to the Indian Ocean island of Mauritius and onwards to Singapore. In addition to this twice-weekly service the airline also operates two flights from Cape Town and two from Durban which route via Johannesburg to Singapore, making it the only non-African airline to operate into all three major South African airports.

Above: Atlas Air 747-200 freighter N523MC taxiing to one of the 'Delta' stands is a good example of the variety of long-haul freighters which visit Johannesburg. Some are operating charters whilst others such as Lufthansa's MD-11Fs and MK Airlines' 747Fs maintain regular scheduled services. Atlas began flying in 1993 with a single 747 freighter and specialises in the operation of cargo services on behalf of many of the world's major airlines. Such is the demand for this work that by the end of 2000 it had become the largest operator of 747 freighters with thirty-seven in service, including twelve new Series -400Fs – impressive growth for an airline without any routes of its own.

Above: Many airlines cover great distances en route to South Africa. For example Qantas flies from Sydney five times a week and Cathay Pacific operates four non-stop flights from Hong Kong to Johannesburg.

Non-scheduled Airlines and Freight Operators

The Republic of South Africa encompasses an area five times the size of the United Kingdom and contains an abundance of natural resources as well as a wealth of attractions for visitors. As a result there is a growing need for the movement of people and cargoes, often to places far removed from the major airports served by scheduled airline services. Whilst some specialist operators such as Court Helicopters have been established for many years, it was the gradual deregulation of the industry from the early-1990s which allowed private enterprise to flourish. A whole range of operators now fulfil these needs using a variety of aircraft types which are able to cope with the tough operating conditions of the southern African region.

Court Helicopters, one of the world's leading helicopter support operators, has its headquarters at Cape Town International Airport although only a small part of its fleet can be found there. Most of the thirty-plus helicopters operate away from base fulfilling contracts in a wide variety of roles which include the support of off-shore oil and diamond production, emergency medical services, rescue services, surveying and passenger charters. Court Helicopters also provides a 24-hours a day supply service to ships as they round the southern tip of Africa off the Cape of Good Hope. This was pioneered by the company's predecessor Autair in September 1968 as the world's first commercial helicopter ship supply service. Here ZS-HVJ, one of five trusty Sikorsky S-61Ns, returns to Court's heliport in Cape Town's busy dock area after supplying a drilling rig temporarily anchored offshore.

A pair of immaculate Convair CV-580s are maintained and flown by Court Air primarily for use in support of the parent company's helicopter operations. Much of the work currently involves transporting crews to Alexander Bay in the north-west corner of South Africa from where they cross to Oranjemund in Namibia for a helicopter flight to an offshore diamond mining vessel. The Convairs, which are the only passenger-carrying examples anywhere in Africa, have been upgraded and refurbished with comfortable 55-seat interiors and are in constant demand for charter work. For example, sports teams and corporate groups are transported around the country and tourist groups are flown to popular destinations such as Victoria Falls. Both Convairs are now approaching fifty years old but with their modest rate of utilisation and good support from Court's in-house engineering facility, replacement is not yet a consideration. If the company's name and livery are familiar to European readers that is because its origins lie with British airline Court Line which collapsed suddenly in 1974. Thankfully its South African helicopter subsidiary survived and has prospered ever since.

Above: ZS-XGZ *Zig-Zag* is one of three immaculate HS-748s operated by Intensive Air, an airline which was founded by an eminent heart surgeon with a passion for aviation. All three 748s have unusual names, the other two are ZS-XGE *Pudding* and ZS-XGY *Muffin*, named after the owner's wife's dogs! Fokker F-28s have recently been added to the fleet and are being used to introduce low-fare scheduled services between Johannesburg and Cape Town.

Above: The two HS-748-2Bs operated by AirQuarius rest at their Lanseria airport base. This tough and dependable 44-seat airliner was designed over forty years ago specifically to operate into basic airstrips with little or no ground support and despite its advancing age the 748 continues to excel at this. Two powerful Rolls-Royce Dart engines provide it with unrivalled payload and range performance from remote African airfields which are often too restrictive for modern turboprops. In addition to the operators shown here, Executive Aerospace operates six HS-748s on charters and scheduled services on behalf of other airlines throughout the Southern African region.

Above: Four veteran Fokker F-27s were acquired by IBU-Air during 1997/8 and are based at Wonderboom Airport near Pretoria. They are used primarily for the carriage of overnight freight, hence the Luft Cargo colour scheme displayed here by ZS-OEK. All four were delivered to the Royal Netherlands Air Force back in 1960 as F-27-300M 'Troopships' and in later years they became very popular airshow performers with their dramatic, almost aerobatic routines.

Above: Passenger-configured short-fuselage Boeing 727-100s are disappearing rapidly throughout the world, so the sight of one of Millionair Charter's ex-American Airlines 727-23s at Johannesburg International is very welcome. Millionair began operating in 1986 and offers a charter service for groups and corporate clients. It also operated scheduled services for Uganda Airlines between Johannesburg, Harare and Entebbe during 2000.

Above: A fine example of business enterprise in South Africa today can be found at Phoebus Apollo Aviation. From its origins as a flight training business in 1986 the company has grown to become a major operator in southern Africa's cargo and passenger charter markets. In addition, Phoebus Apollo's flying school and extensive engineering facilities are well known throughout the world and attract many customers. The airline's distinctive blue and gold livery is displayed on Douglas C-54 Skymaster ZS-PAI seen taxiing at its Rand Airport base. Named *Apollo* it is one of two airworthy Skymasters in the fleet, both of which are USAF veterans from 1945.

Above: Following the pattern of many local airlines Phoebus Apollo's first large aircraft was, of course, a Dakota. This particular C-47A ZS-DIW *Pegasus* has served southern African operators continually since joining the South African Air Force in 1944.

Above: This truly vintage airliner is one of the first Pratt & Whitney powered DC-3 Dakotas built as a 'Douglas Sleeper Transport' for United Airlines in 1937. After a hardworking career it was rescued by the owner of Phoebus Apollo from Mozambique in 1997 and flown to Rand where the airline's workshops began a thorough restoration programme. The Dakota will be equipped with original-design leather seats and Phoebus Apollo plans to use it to operate leisurely and luxurious ten-day air-cruises to Europe carrying just twenty lucky passengers. The aim is to recreate some of the romance and adventure of early long-haul travel with up to four hours of flying on most days and night-stops at places of interest each night. The owner is sparing no expense in his quest to make this the finest Dakota anywhere in the world and once in service it will undoubtedly be the oldest airliner ever to operate regular long-haul services.

Left: Pratt & Whitney Twin Wasp engines from all over the world are overhauled in Phoebus Apollo's workshops. This example is about to undergo performance checks on the company's purpose-built test rig before being returned to service. It is one of up to thirty such engines which emerge in as good as new condition each year.

Although this Dakota will never take to the air again, a new use has been found for it as a 'gate guard' at Phoebus Apollo's Rand Airport headquarters.

Sixty-five years after the legendary Douglas DC-3 Dakota first flew, many fine examples can still be found giving valuable service in South Africa. During a recent tour of Johannesburg's airfields no less than thirty were counted, almost all of which were either air-worthy or awaiting restoration. Although it was originally designed as a sleeper transport for the American transcontinental market, the Dakota was built with many features which still today make it an ideal transport for Africa's harsh conditions. In fact, with the ability to operate from almost any airstrip combined with a rugged but easily maintained structure, the Dakota still has no equal.

Stored Douglas DC-6BF 9Q-CJX frames one of Debon-Air Tours' Dakotas during a quiet moment at Rand Airport (*top*). Another Dakota seen in the company of Rand's population of DC-6s is ZS-DRJ (*above*) which was restored to flying condition in 2000 following a period out of service.

Above: At the end of a ten-hour flight from northern Angola long-nosed DC-3 ZS-LVR with *Memphis Belle* titles rests on the apron at Lanseria. Sadly this Dakota was badly damaged by a ground fire in February 2000.

Above: Sporting an immaculate civilian colour scheme, J.A.M. Air's Andover C1 shows no trace of its thirty years of service with the Royal Air Force and Royal New Zealand Air Force. The features which made the Andover an excellent tactical freighter are exactly those which are required for its new role with civilian cargo carriers and relief agencies in Africa, i.e. excellent short-field performance and self-sufficiency plus a kneeling undercarriage and drop-down rear ramp for ease of loading. Andovers are often seen at Lanseria, such as this example which carries the Equatorial Guinea registration 3C-JJX.

By the dawn of the new century only a handful of the 282 Caravelles produced by Sud Aviation/Aerospatiale between 1958 and 1972 remained airworthy. Two of these were at Rand Airport during 1999, both late-model 11Rs equipped with large freight doors and strengthened floors for the carriage of passengers and freight. They were originally delivered to Air Congo in 1967/68 and were sold to the French Air Force for support work in the South Pacific from 1976 to 1996. These photographs show one of the Caravelles which arrived at Rand registered 9Q-CNA, still in basic French Air Force colours and with Malu Aviation titles. By October 1999 it had been repainted for Gabon Express as 3D-CNA although it initially entered service as a freighter with Central African Cargo. Sistership 3D-SEP was delivered to Libreville where it has been operating the scheduled services of Gabon Express since July 1999.

This Rwanda-registered Convair 580 freighter at Lanseria in September 2000 is in fact one of a small batch of Canadair CC-109 Cosmopolitans built for the Royal Canadian Air Force in 1960. After their retirement in 1994 the seven remaining Cosmopolitans were stored in Canada and so far this is the only one to have found new employment. It arrived at Rand early in 2000 and was registered 5Y-BNV before entering service with Central African Cargo as 9XR-NC.

Ex-Soviet freighters are not as common in South Africa as they were several years ago, as the authorities have clamped down on some of their less reputable operators. However, Antonov's rugged and powerful turboprop freighters are ideally suited to the harsh African conditions and properly operated examples can still be found, particularly at Lanseria where three Moldovan-registered Antonovs are shown awaiting their next assignments (*above*). Two are An-32s with their distinctive rear loading ramps, the third is an An-24RV. Although both types originate from the same family there are major differences between the An-24 and -32. The An-32 has much more powerful engines which give it excellent performance from hot and high airfields plus overwing nacelles which keep the propellers clear of the ground. Depicted opposite are An-24RV ER-AEZ (*top*) and Russian An-32, RA-29120 (*bottom*). Both aircraft were operated on lease by Africa Cargo Airlines.

A long way from home is another Moldovan freighter, Sud Aerocargo's Antonov An-12B ER-ACK, resting between assignments at Johannesburg International's Cargo Centre (*top*). Also visiting Johannesburg was Ukrainian Cargo Airways' Il-76MD freighter UR-UCL, which was collecting cargo on behalf of the United Nations (*above*).

ZS-OGE, a CASA-235 of Luftmeister Air, taxiing at Johannesburg
International during May 1999.

A selection of classic Boeing jet airliners can usually be seen visiting South Africa's airports, such as 727-35 TN-AFY of Trans Air Congo (*above*) at Lanseria and Grecoair's 707-336C 5Y-BNJ (*top*) at Johannesburg International. They are typical of the many early jets which have found new employment in Africa after being replaced with more modern types by their original owners. Both began their long careers within days of each other back in November 1967, the 727 with American Airlines as N1957, the 707 with BOAC and later British Airways as G-ATWV.

Stored, Undergoing Rebuild or Maintenance

The airfields around Johannesburg and Pretoria host what is undoubtedly the best selection of classic western transport aircraft remaining in existence today. Whilst the more active members of this constantly changing population are illustrated on other pages, this section focuses on those which are currently out of service. Some of them are undergoing long-term maintenance or a complete rebuild and others are just parked up waiting for their next contract. Only a few have been grounded forever.

One of many activities which take place at Rand Airport is the maintenance and storage of old airliners, most of which have seen service elsewhere in Africa as freighters. Visitors to the roof-terrace or 'Le Piston' restaurant in the airport's nostalgic old terminal building can admire a splendid line-up of veteran airliners such as those illustrated opposite.

Opposite and top: Four of the seven DC-4s operated by the South African Air Force until 1994 can still be found in the Johannesburg area. Two are flown regularly with the South African Historic Flight and one is kept in a taxyable condition by the Air Force Museum at Swartkop. The fourth, currently registered in Swaziland as 3D-JHL, has been parked at Rand for several years although it does fly an occasional freight charter.

Above: This immaculate freighter is DC-6A EL-WIL, which has been parked at Rand Airport for the last four years. Hopefully this will prove to be just a temporary pause in the aircraft's long career, which began with its delivery to the USAF as a C-118A Liftmaster in 1955. During the last two decades it has served a variety of civil operators in the USA, Canada, Guatemala and Venezuela as well as Africa.

Above: One of five DC-6s stored at Rand during 1998 was Transair Cargo's 9Q-CJE. During November of that year it was re-registered ZS-XXX and departed for the short ferry flight to Johannesburg International to join the South African Airways Historic Flight. The DC-6BF has subsequently moved on to storage at Swartkop where it is maintained in a potentially flyable condition. Prior to its arrival in Africa during 1980 this DC-6 was operated for a short time by Air Atlantique with the appropriate British registration G-SIXB.

Above: These smart looking DC-6s were taken out of storage in Florida during 1996 and flown across the Atlantic to haul freight in central Africa. They were registered to Service Air as 9Q-CYO and 9Q-CGZ, but following an overhaul and repaint they have remained idle at Rand since 1998. Several such piston-engined veterans have been parked out of use for the last few years after escaping from areas of Africa which have been ravaged by wars. Although they are excellent freighters and are capable of many more years of productive use, their future employment prospects are now constrained by growing shortages of AVGAS fuel in many places.

Aero Air's C-47A Dakota ZS-NTE, previously 6873 of the South African Air Force, undergoes a leisurely refurbishment and conversion for civilian flying at Rand Airport. The engines warming up in the foreground belong to Phoebus Apollo's magnificent Skymaster ZS-PAI.

Above: Andover C1 9Q-CPW, parked alongside Dakota ZS-PTG at Rand Airport during January 2000, is another example of the many ex-military freighters which are now in widespread use throughout Africa. A total of thirty-one Andover C1s were built by Hawker Siddeley for the Royal Air Force during 1966/67, ten of which were sold to the Royal New Zealand Air Force in 1976. By the mid-1990s most Andovers had been retired from military service but thanks to their unrivalled ability to operate out of rough airstrips more than one third of the total built have subsequently found work in Africa.

Above: A genuine 'Hangar Queen' is this ex-Madagascar Government VIP-configured HS-748 which has been stored at Rand since an overhaul was abandoned several years ago. Whilst its ownership was debated in the courts, 5R-MUT sat in a hangar where it was stripped of engines and other useful parts with its chances of a rebuild to flying condition gradually fading.

Unusual types can often be found amongst the stored DC-4s and -6s at Rand such as this Antonov An-26 painted with the Liberian registration EL-AHO. It was seen during May 1999 wearing basic Aeroflot colours and small 'Air Angol' stickers, which suggest that it had recently seen service in Angola.

Amongst the rolling hills of the veld is Lanseria Airport, a thriving centre for the business and general aviation aircraft which serve Johannesburg and Pretoria. However, in amongst the hangars full of exotically-registered executive aircraft are some real airliner treasures such as Douglas C-54 EL-AWX and DC-6 EL-WNH (*bottom, background*). Photographed in October 1998 EL-AWX had recently returned from service with one of the aid organisations which assist the victims of war, political troubles and natural disasters across Africa. Despite having first flown over fifty years ago the old Skymaster was not yet ready for retirement and, following a thorough overhaul it entered service with Phoebus Apollo during 2000 as ZS-PAJ.

Could this be a scene from the dreams of a prop-enthusiast? A classic piston-engined airliner parked alongside a landscaped garden complete with a pool and bathed in hot African sunshine! The airliner is in fact one of the oldest DC-6s remaining today, a fifty-year old veteran registered EL-WNH. Despite having been parked out of service at Lanseria since 1997, it remains in a potentially flyable condition.

The world's first turbine-powered passenger airliner was the Vickers Viscount, which went on to become the most successful airliner ever built in Britain. During the 1950s and '60s Viscounts equipped many of the world's major airlines and were familiar sights throughout southern Africa for many years with carriers such as SAA and Air Zimbabwe. However, that was not the end of the story as five Viscounts were delivered from Europe to South Africa during 1997 and 1999 and these are now the last commercially-operated examples of the type. Three arrived at Lanseria for Heli Jet Aviation including all-red Viscount 806 freighter G-PFBT, seen here (*top*) behind G-APEY. Whilst G-PFBT has remained out of use as a source of spare parts, G-APEY has flown extensively in Angola, Zimbabwe and Gabon, registered 3C-PBH. Meanwhile G-BFZL (*bottom*) has undergone a complete overhaul in preparation for its return to service.

The other two Viscounts, both of which entered service back in 1957 with British European Airways, arrived at Wonderboom Airport during 1999. They also wore a dramatic red colour scheme, clear evidence of their previous use by British World Airlines for overnight postal delivery services in the UK. These Viscount 802s are in superb condition and make excellent freighters with their ability to uplift eight-tonne payloads. However maintenance costs – particularly for the engines and propellers – are high and some certification problems have been encountered, so they have seen very little flying since their arrival in South Africa. This Viscount painted as 3D-PFI is ex G-OPFI, whilst sistership 3D-OHM was previously G-AOHM.

Above: Rwanda Airlines' One-Eleven 9XR-RA arrived at Lanseria during August 2000 for engineering work with One-Eleven specialist Nationwide Airlines. This Series -201, which is used primarily as a government transport, was originally built for British United Airways as G-ASJG back in 1964 and is the second-oldest One-Eleven remaining in the world today.

Above: Honduran-registered Lockheed L-188A Electra HR-AMM has seen little flying since its retirement from passenger service with Varig of Brazil in 1992. However, it still remains intact and potentially airworthy at Lanseria whilst a buyer is sought. Unfortunately the lack of a cargo door may result in the Electra being dismantled to provide spares for other examples, which continue to provide valuable service as freighters elsewhere in the world.

Amongst the many modern helicopters at Lanseria stored SA321L Super Frelon ZS-HTN with 'Com Jet' titles certainly stands out as something from a much earlier age!

One of Rossair's two AMI Turbo DC-3s running up a Pratt & Whitney PT6A turboprop at its Lanseria base. The longer fuselage of the re-engined Dakota is clearly visible.

Top: Although C-47TP Turbo Dakota 6892 at Wonderboom in October 1998 was wearing full South African Air Force markings, it was awaiting delivery to its new American owner Dodson Aviation as N195RD. *Bottom*: Nearby, a securely fenced-off compound contained another eight Dakotas, all dismantled and awaiting shipment to the USA to be refurbished and sold.

One of only three Aviation Traders Carvairs to survive from the twenty-one built was parked for some time at Wonderboom Airport to the north of Pretoria. Previously registered N5459M, the Carvair has spent most of the last twenty years out of service following the failure of several freight-hauling enterprises, initially in New Zealand, then Honolulu and finally, since 1996, in South Africa. Despite being well cared for during that time little interest was shown in the unique capabilities of this heavily modified DC-4. In November 2000 it left for Johannesburg then flew north to face an uncertain future elsewhere in Africa.

The tiny airfield at Brakpan-Benoni in the outlying suburbs of Johannesburg is used by Interocean Airways for maintenance work on its fleet. During recent years Dakotas and Skymasters have been regular visitors for engine changes, but usually the only large aircraft to be seen are the airfield's more permanent residents – two derelict de Havilland Canada Caribous, N544Y and C9-ATE.

Government and Private Aviation

South Africa has a large and thriving population of privately-owned aircraft ranging from small sport and touring aircraft to the sophisticated executive transports of large corporations. Various Government agencies also operate aircraft in specialised roles.

Above: The South African Directorate of Civil Aviation maintains a base at Johannesburg International Airport for a fleet which consists mainly of modern aircraft types. Until recently, however, two notable exceptions were an immaculate de Havilland Canada DHC-2 Beaver ZS-CAJ and DC-3C Dakota ZS-CAI (*opposite*). Sadly, the Beaver was sold in Canada in June 2000 and the Dakota has also been offered for sale. Prior to its departure, the Beaver's impressive capabilities as a bush transport were put to good use during an airlift to provide relief to the people of Mozambique following disastrous flooding across the country early in 2000.

Above: Another small transport renowned for its short take-off and landing capabilities and excellent low-speed handling is the Swiss Pilatus PC-6 Turbo Porter. With a powerful Pratt & Whitney PT-6A turboprop engine and room to accommodate up to ten passengers, Turbo Porter ZS-NIT makes an ideal spotter and utility aircraft for the South African Police Service.

These Gulfstream Fours (*opposite*) serve to illustrate the corporate and government-operated aircraft which can be seen at Johannesburg. ZS-NMO is locally-based with the Anglo American Corporation whereas JY-RAY was operated for the government of the Hashemite Kingdom of Jordan. The Gulfstream Four is an impressive performer, capable of flying over 4,000 miles non-stop thanks to its two powerful Rolls-Royce Tay turbofans. It was introduced in 1985 as the latest and much improved version of a long-running family of executive aircraft descended from the original Dart-powered Grumman Gulfstream One, which first flew as long ago as 1958. ZS-ONO at Rand is one of several Gulfstream Ones still active in southern Africa (*above*).

Lanseria Airport offers a convenient and secure base for the many executive aircraft which serve both Johannesburg and the country's administrative capital Pretoria. Examples are Challenger 601 ZS-NKD and Lear Jet 31A ZS-AGT (*top*) and Lear Jet 35A ZS-DJB and Challenger 604 ZS-DGB (*bottom*).

Above: The orange glow from a spectacular South African sunset illuminates ExecuJet Air Charter's Lear Jet 31A ZS-OML.

Above: A very popular type in South African skies for sport flying is the amazing Pitts Special. This tiny but very agile biplane revolutionised the world of aerobatics and remains in production today well over fifty years after the original prototype first took to the air.

Unusual examples of privately-owned aircraft were three Gabon-registered Fouga CM-170 Magisters which were overhauled at Rand Airport during 1999. These ageing 'warbirds' are French-designed two-seat trainers, although they are also capable of carrying light armaments. All three had served with the Austrian Air force until 1976 before joining the Gabon Presidential Guard as 366, 367 and 368. They left Rand in August 1999 and headed north on delivery to a new owner.

Aircraft Preservation

South Africa has some of the most experienced and sophisticated aircraft preservation groups to be found anywhere in the world. Classic airliners have been operated successfully for many years and the Air Force maintains airworthy examples of several of its older types. The civilian warbird scene is also thriving with many new types being brought into the country in recent years, most notably the incredible fast-jets of Cape Town's Thunder City Entertainments.

The South African Historic Flight (previously the South African Airways Historic Flight) is very well known for pioneering the commercial use of restored airliners. Two fully operational and luxuriously appointed Douglas DC-4 Skymasters and a Dakota have been used for many years to perform charters, which range from local one-hour 'Champagne specials' and safari trips to ambitious trans-continental expeditions. The Skymasters were both delivered new to South African Airways in 1946/7 and have spent their entire operational careers with southern African operators. After twenty years of worldwide airline service with SAA they transferred to the South African Air Force for thirty years of tough duty with Number 44 Squadron. Finally ZS-BMH (*opposite*), which was the last DC-4 ever built, joined the Historic Flight's operational fleet in 1993 followed by ZS-AUB (*above*) in 1997.

Until 1999 the Historic Flight and associated Museum were housed in South African Airways' engineering base at Johannesburg International Airport where both DC-4s shared a hangar with two ex-South African Air Force Dakotas. ZS-BXF, shown here, has been active with the Historic Flight since October 1993 whilst ZS-BXJ, which can just be seen in the back of the hangar (*opposite*) has been undergoing a complete rebuild for several years. However, during 1998/9 SAA decided to reclaim its facilities and sever all links with the group, forcing it to move to Swartkop Air Force Base near Pretoria. Although good facilities were obtained at Swartkop the separation from SAA's personnel and facilities has made the operation of these historic veterans much more difficult and costly.

The Historic Flight's airliners have all been painted in different colour schemes to represent various stages in South African Airways' past. These three examples are DC-4 ZS-BMH in the airline's 1950s scheme, DC-4 ZS-AUB in late-60s orange and Dakota ZS-BXF which wears blue and silver colours from the early postwar years.

Two airliners which will never take to the air again are the Museum's Lockheed L-1649A Starliner and Vickers Viking. With its distinctive triple-fin arrangement the Starliner is unmistakably a member of the Constellation family. In fact it was the ultimate development, which utilised some of the most powerful piston-engines ever built in the quest for non-stop intercontinental range. Unfortunately for Lockheed, the first jets were about to enter service so only forty-three of these elegant airliners were ever built. ZS-DVJ was delivered to Lufthansa in 1958 and served Trek Airways and Luxair on flights between Europe and South Africa from 1964 until 1969, when it was retired at Johannesburg. One last flight took the Starliner to Wonderboom in 1971 for use as a restaurant, but these plans came to nothing and the aircraft was left to deteriorate. In 1979 a group from SAA dismantled the Starliner and returned it to Johannesburg by road, a difficult task which imposed such heavy stresses on the airframe that it would never be able to fly again. Restoration to static condition began in 1984 and within four years the Starliner had been reassembled and painted. Since then a group of keen volunteers has worked to refurbish the interior for public access but for now this rare and beautiful airliner remains stranded in the SAA base.

Also left behind at Johannesburg is Vickers Viking 1A ZS-DKH, which is in a very poor condition following many years in the open. This early production Viking was delivered to British European Airways in 1946 then served several charter carriers until its acquisition by Trek Airways in 1954. Protea Airways was the Viking's final operator before its retirement in the early '60s and subsequent display on top of 'Vic's Viking Garage' near Johannesburg. Although SAA did not operate this particular aircraft it was acquired to represent the eight Vikings flown by the airline fifty years ago. It will, however, take many years of dedicated work to restore the Viking to anything like its former glory.

Other preserved airliners include a de Havilland Dove (*above*), Lockheed Lodestar and airworthy Junkers Ju-52 ZS-AFA (*top*) which was the first aircraft operated by the Historic Flight. The Ju-52 is actually a Spanish-built CASA 352L, purchased from a warbird dealer in the UK during 1980 and shipped to South Africa. After a complete rebuild the old tri-motor was ready to take part in

SAA's fiftieth anniversary celebrations in February 1984 where it represented the Ju-52s flown by the airline before World War Two. The success of this operation led to the creation of the Historic Flight, but in recent years the Ju-52's flying has been severely restricted by a shortage of tyres.

South African Air Force Museum

The South African Air Force is particularly proud of its long history as the second-oldest independent air force in the world. Over the years an impressive collection of retired aircraft has been assembled at locations across the country and great efforts have been made to acquire and restore airframes to fill any significant gaps. The SAAF Museum is based at Swartkop, a recently de-activated Air Force Base near Pretoria, which was home to the first flying units back in the early 1920s. This historic airfield is now dedicated to the preservation of the nation's aviation heritage,

much of it contained within the original hangars and buildings from those early days. Examples of most types operated during the last fifty years are on display and many are kept in flying condition. The collection of combat types is particularly impressive and includes examples of the Mustang, Sabre, Buccaneer, Canberra and several different Mirage variants. Larger exhibits include C-47 Dakotas, a C-54 Skymaster and Avro Shackleton maritime reconnaissance aircraft.

Above: One of the greatest achievements of the SAAF Museum has been to maintain examples of the maritime reconnaissance Avro Shackleton in airworthy condition. The last of Number 35 Squadron's eight Shackleton MR3s were retired in December 1984 and put on display as illustrated here by 1716 and 1721 at Swartkop in 1993. 1716 was subsequently brought back to flying condition for display purposes but was written off in July 1994

whilst en route from Cape Town to the UK. The Shackleton had developed serious engine and propeller problems which led to a forced landing in the western Sahara desert, thankfully without any casualties. Another Shackleton, 1722, replaced it and has been operated by 35 Squadron for the SAAF Museum. However, time is literally running out for what may be the last Shackleton to fly as it now has very few airframe hours remaining.

The SAAF Museum acquired an ex-Dominican Air Force P-51D Mustang from the USA in 1987 to fill a gap in its collection. After a lengthy rebuild the Mustang returned to the air in October 1998 and now flies regularly wearing the markings of '325', a Number 2 Squadron aircraft named *Patsy Dawn* which served in Korea during the early 1950s.

Another recently completed restoration is this Sabre Mk.6 which flew again in March 2000 after a three-year rebuild. Number 367 is one of thirty-four Canadian-built Sabres flown by the SAAF during the 1950s. It has recently been painted in the markings of Number 2 Squadron *The Flying Cheetahs*.

Two Dassault Mirage 3s are maintained and flown as examples of the SAAF's first Mach-2 capable aircraft. These potent fighters are now very rare as most air forces have either retired their Mirage 3s or rebuilt them to produce substantially different aircraft such as South Africa's own Cheetah. They are very popular with airshow audiences, performing fast and noisy routines with the liberal use of reheat on the aircraft's powerful Atar turbojet. Mirage 3CZ 800, an interceptor named *Black Widow*, wears a black and gold livery whereas 817, a two-seat Mirage 3BZ named *Skydancer*, displays the black, red, green, blue and gold colours of the South African flag.

Although the RAF never actually flew an all-black Lightning, ZU-BBD looks magnificent in this livery. In addition to enhancing its appearance this paint-scheme has a practical purpose as it serves to make the aircraft highly visible in the air. To complete each Lightning's restoration, accurate squadron markings from the type's final operational days are being applied. T5 ZU-BBD carries the markings of the last unit to operate Lightnings, No. 11 Squadron's pair of eagles. The second two-seater ZU-BEX flies with a highly polished natural metal finish typical of the Lightning's early days and displays small Lightning Training Flight tail markings. Of the F6s ZU-BEW (XR773) will retain the two-tone grey air defence livery from its last days with the RAF and ZU-BEY (XP693), which was always a trials aircraft with British Aerospace, will also emerge with a natural metal finish.

In addition to the world's only airworthy Lightnings, Thunder City also has the last two operational Buccaneers, an aircraft which is widely acknowledged to have been one of the greatest low-level, all-weather strike aircraft ever built. The mighty Blackburn Buccaneer, however, is not a new shape in South Africa's skies as this was the only country other than Britain ever to have operated the type. Sixteen Buccaneer S50s were bought for the South African Air Force during the mid-1960s and were flown by Number 24 Squadron until a shortage of spares grounded the last ones in June 1991. The final RAF Buccaneers were also prematurely retired with the last two squadrons losing their aircraft by 1994. Just two Buccaneers then remained in service, flying as weapons release trials aircraft until they were acquired by Mike Beachy Head in 1996 and flown to South Africa. Both aircraft were found to be in exceptional condition and, as a result of having spent their entire twenty year careers as trials aircraft, had accumulated very few flying hours. Thunder City soon obtained full civilian certificates of airworthiness for the Buccaneers and expects to fly them for many more years.

The Buccaneer's reputation for being solidly built and for being very stable at low level makes it a perfect partner to the somewhat more lively Lightning in the Thunder City fleet. Clients can sample an exhilarating low-level flight through the valleys in a Buccaneer or a high-speed dash at high altitude in a Lightning. The ultimate package however begins with two flights in a Hunter leading to two flights in a Buccaneer and finally a supersonic sortie in the Lightning!

A glimpse inside Thunder City's unassuming AMARC (Aircraft Maintenance and Restoration Centre) hangar at Cape Town reveals an amazing sight – a collection of veteran British combat jets which would not have been out of place on many RAF bases twenty years ago. During June 2000 no less than four Lightnings, four Hunters, two Buccaneers and a Strikemaster were present, all of which were either airworthy or waiting to be restored. Thunder City is now implementing ambitious plans to build an entertainment centre which will recreate the atmosphere and excitement of modern military aircraft operations. Realistic simulations will, for example, take visitors onto the flight deck of a US Navy aircraft carrier or into the forward operating base of an RAF Harrier detachment. Many more aircraft will join the collection, which will confirm Cape Town's position as an important centre for the preservation and display of retired military aircraft. Thunder City is investigating extensions to the operating fleet with exciting types such as the F-4 Phantom, F-14 Tomcat and MiG-29 'Fulcrum' strong possibilities.

PBY-5A Catalina C-FPQO is currently being refurbished at Rand
Airport for charter work in southern Africa. The exterior has been
finished in a smart blue and white scheme and work is underway
to fit out the interior.

Two very different classic aircraft sharing the apron at Lanseria in October 1998 were Vickers Viscount G-BFZL and Beech Staggerwing ZS-AJT (*top*). The Staggerwing is a fine example of the many privately-owned vintage aircraft which are lovingly cared for and flown throughout South Africa. Another good example is Tiger Moth ZS-BGN shown taxiing at Rand after an early morning flight (*above*).

The only Spitfire currently airworthy in South Africa is TE566 (ZU-SPT), a Mark IX similar to those which saw extensive service with the SAAF during and after the Second World War. Private owner Andrew Torr brought the Spitfire from the UK in 1998. It is based at Swartkop and regularly takes part in airshows alongside aircraft of the SAAF Museum.

One of the most successful aircraft ever to emerge from the former Czechoslovakia was the Aero L-29 Delfin (Dolphin), a rugged trainer which served the air forces of most Warsaw Pact countries from the mid-1960s. Over 3,600 Delfins were eventually built, some of which found their way to various African air forces. In recent years, private warbird owners have been attracted by the type's simple construction and good handling qualities as well as the availability of good examples such as ZU-AUW seen here.

The SAAF finally retired its last fifty Harvard trainers in 1995. Although some were sold overseas, particularly in the United States, most have remained in South Africa with private owners. The examples shown here are ZU-AOR *Nellie* and the Peugeot Lions aerobatic display team Harvards which retain their SAAF colours.

South African Air Force

The South African Air Force (SAAF) has emerged from difficult times during the 1970/80s into a completely new era, one which has brought with it a new set of problems. In November 1977 a United Nations arms embargo was introduced, which forced the SAAF to rely heavily on local industry for its very survival. Advanced technologies were developed and innovative solutions were employed to enhance the effectiveness of existing aircraft. New types such as the Rooivalk attack helicopter were also developed out of this necessity. After the removal of these restrictions in the 1990s several overseas orders were placed, which will lead to a range of modern equipment entering service over the next few years. However, the SAAF now faces the same challenge as Air Forces all over the world as it struggles to finance the huge cost of this re-equipment from a severely restricted budget. During the last decade many aircraft types have been retired and flying hours have been drastically reduced in order to save costs. Despite this the SAAF, which celebrated its eightieth anniversary during 2000, is still the most potent force in the region and continues to maintain a wide range of operational capabilities. Once the new Gripens, Hawks and advanced helicopters are in service this position will have been further strengthened.

Number 35 Squadron operates substantially upgraded versions of the venerable C-47 Dakota from Cape Town International Airport. Their missions include maritime reconnaissance and rescue work over the oceans around the Cape plus general transport, target towing and parachute training. A variety of liveries reflect these different roles such as 6875 (*above*) which is used as a VIP transport and 6877 (*opposite*), which is equipped for maritime reconnaissance. The SAAF has operated Dakotas continuously since 1943 making it one of the longest-ever users of the type. Despite their age, however, the Dakotas are still very capable, particularly since their conversion to turboprop power. This was performed locally in South Africa during the 1990s and involved replacing the original Pratt & Whitney Twin Wasp piston engines with PT-6As from the same manufacturer. New five-blade propellers were also fitted and the fuselage was extended by forty inches. The end result is a greatly improved aircraft which is considerably cheaper to operate and is no longer dependent upon dwindling supplies of AVGAS fuel. It also offers much better performance, increased capacity, and is more reliable. Further upgrades to the mission equipment are now being installed which should ensure that the dozen remaining C-47TP Turbo Dakotas continue to serve the Air Force for many more years.

The SAAF's prime combat aircraft is currently the Cheetah, a locally modified version of the veteran Dassault Mirage 3. During the 1980s, when the purchase of new fighters from abroad was impossible, Atlas (now Denel Aerospace) developed an upgrade package for the Air Force's Mirages which had been in service since the 1960s. Major modifications included the fitting of canard lifting surfaces and wing leading-edge extensions to improve agility, new avionics and weaponry plus structural changes to prolong the aircraft lives. The first Cheetah entered service in 1987 and up to sixty conversions have subsequently been performed. Number 2 Squadron currently operates the type from its base at Louis Trichardt AFB in the north-east corner of South Africa. Although the Cheetah remains a potent interceptor it will be replaced over the next ten years by one of the most advanced fighters available today, the Saab Gripen.

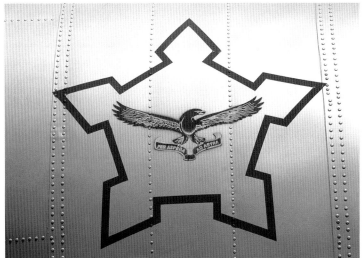

The Lockheed C-130B Hercules has been the SAAF's transport workhorse since 1963 when seven were acquired. Over thirty years later and with no money available for replacements the Air Force acquired five redundant US military C-130Bs and Fs and embarked upon a major update programme for its fleet. The work is being carried out by Denel in association with Marshall Aerospace in the UK and aims to upgrade and standardise the fleet as well as to extend the useful life of each aircraft by another thirty years. By 2002, Number 28 Squadron at Waterkloof expects to have received the last of its fully-updated Hercules.

The SAAF's main transport helicopter is the Atlas Oryx, a significantly modified licence-built derivative of the Aerospatiale Puma. Approximately fifty Oryx were delivered from 1988 replacing Super Frelons and Pumas. Here 1225 of Number 17 Squadron gives some brave soldiers a lift (*opposite*)! SAAF helicopter crews were given the opportunity to put their flying skills to good use early in 2000 when they rescued hundreds of people from Mozambique's devastating floods.

The AH-2 Rooivalk or Red Kestrel has entered service after a long
drawn out programme to develop an indigenous attack helicopter
for the SAAF. Experimental conversions of Alouette 3 and Pumas
first appeared during the 1980s and led to the first flight of a prototype Rooivalk in February 1990. The first production machine was
delivered to Number 16 Squadron at Bloemspruit in October 1999
and all twelve are expected to be in service by 2001.

The SAAF has ordered nine two-seat Saab JAS-39 Gripen (Griffin)
fighters in the first stage of a programme to replace its ageing
Cheetahs. They will enter service from 2006 and, if existing
options are confirmed, a second batch of nineteen single-seaters
will eventually join them. South Africa will be the second operator of the Gripen following the Swedish Air Force which has flown
the type since 1993. The Swedish example shown here took part
in the SAAF's eightieth anniversary celebrations at Waterkloof
during September 2000. Its impressive display of agility gave the
Air Force a taste of what to expect in the not too distant future.

With the advanced Gripen due to enter service, the SAAF urgently needs a more capable lead-in fighter trainer to replace its obsolete Atlas Impalas. To satisfy this requirement twelve British Aerospace Hawk 120s will arrive from 2005 and options are held for another twelve. As far as possible the Hawks will have their cockpit systems designed to replicate those of the Gripen in order to simplify the training process. They will also be capable of carrying a wide range of armaments, although the Air Force only plans to use them as trainers. Initial pilot training will be conducted on the turboprop Pilatus PC-7 Astra leading on to the Hawk and ultimately, for the lucky few, to the Gripen. The trainers illustrated here are: a pair of PC-7s flown by the SAAF's Silver Falcons display team (*opposite top*), Impala Mk2 1063 painted with a special 'gannet' livery derived from the unit badge of No.85 Air Combat School (*opposite bottom*) and a Zimbabwe Air Force two-seat Hawk 60 (*above*) similar to those on order for the SAAF which was displayed at Waterkloof in September 2000.

A variety of small to medium sized transport aircraft are flown by the SAAF. Examples include: 748, a Cessna 185E flown by 44 Squadron (*opposite top*), 8030 a Pilatus PC-12 of Number 41 Squadron (*opposite bottom*) and ZS-LPE a Hawker Siddeley HS125-400B 'Mercurius' of Number 111 Squadron (*above*).

Index of Aircraft Types